The Service Desk Handbook

A guide to service desk implementation,
management and support

The Service Desk Handbook

A guide to service desk implementation,
management and support

SANJAY NAIR

IT Governance Publishing

IT Governance Publishing Ltd
Unit 3, Clive Court
Bartholomew's Walk
Cambridgeshire Business Park
Ely, Cambridgeshire
CB7 4EA
United Kingdom
www.itgovernancepublishing.co.uk

First published in the United Kingdom in 2020 by IT Governance Publishing.

ISBN 978-1-78778-235-8

Dedicated to my parents,

for their prayers and unwavering belief in all my endeavours, big and small.

ABOUT THE AUTHOR

Sanjay Nair is an IT service management (ITSM) professional currently working as a service desk manager in Kuwait. He has over 23 years of experience in the field of IT operations, with a primary focus on the end user support domain. Over the past 8 years, he has been coaching and mentoring service desk teams within the banking and aviation industries, with ITIL® at the forefront of daily operations.

Sanjay has written this book with the intention of providing operational guidance for implementing, managing and supporting service desks in the enterprise. The book will assist service desk teams in adopting ITIL® to accomplish their tasks whilst making the necessary adaptations as per their organisation's needs.

PROLOGUE

So, why did I decide to write this book? The answer is that while there is tons of information on the various aspects of the service desk on the Internet, researching each topic and compiling the required content can take a considerable amount of time and effort.

I am hoping that the topics I cover in this book, along with the samples and templates, provide readers with a reference point for the setup and smooth running of service desk operations in any organisation, irrespective of its size or nature of business, without the hassles of searching for the basics on the boundless highway that is the Internet.

In an already agile world which places more importance on actual work done than comprehensive documentation, this book might seem a little out of place. However, I believe that good practices and related documents will always provide a firm foundation for consistent delivery of services.

ACKNOWLEDGEMENTS

To those who have this book in their hands, it will hopefully serve its purpose and help you (and your teams) become more organised and productive. But for me, it is more than that. This is the fulfilment of a dream, an item ticked off my bucket list, and for that I am forever grateful to the people mentioned below.

First and foremost, I would like to thank my dear friends at Keralite Engineers Association (Kuwait) for constantly encouraging and appreciating the articles that I wrote over the years. A handful of these friends have been with me throughout the years, proofreading my work, suggesting ways to improve it and egging me on to eventually get a book published.

A special mention must go to my former co-columnists at *Rousing The Kop,* a blog dedicated to Liverpool Football Club, who helped develop my passion for writing further.

I have keener eyes at home to thank as well, my family, for giving me honest and impartial feedback and making sure that I stay grounded at all times.

I would also like to thank David Barrow and Michael Walker for their time and effort in providing invaluable feedback to fine-tune the contents of this book.

Tons of gratitude goes out to Nicola Day, production editor at IT Governance Publishing Ltd, for guiding me through this journey and helping see my dream to fruition.

Acknowledgements

However, the biggest appreciations and obligations are reserved for service desk teams, past and present, that I have had the pleasure to be a part of. It is their contributions at work that motivated me to write this book. Their sincerity, dedication to the job at hand, and willingness to constantly learn and improve themselves will always be a source of inspiration to me.

CONTENTS

Chapter 1: What is a service desk? 1
  Mission and vision statements 2
  The environment 2
Chapter 2: Planning for a service desk 7
  1. Type of support experience you want to deliver 7
  2. Staffing requirements 7
  3. Well-defined categorisation and prioritisation 8
  4. Service level agreements (SLAs) 8
  5. Knowledge base and self-service portal 8
  6. Track and improve on key metrics 9
Chapter 3: Telephony and ITSM tools 11
  Telephony 11
  ITSM tool 12
  ITSM configuration 14
Chapter 4: The service desk team 17
  Respect and integrity 17
  Teamwork 17
  Quality service and performance 17
  Efficient and proactive 18
  Single point of contact 18
  The service desk agent 18
  The service desk manager 21
Chapter 5: Documentation 25
  Standard operating procedure manual (SOP) 25
  Knowledge base (solution database) 26
  Process documents 27
  Responsibilities of an incident manager 32
  RACI matrix 33
  RACI matrix 39

Contents

Responsibilities of a problem manager 45
RACI matrix 46
Operational level agreement (OLA) 50
Service catalogue 51
Service request approval matrix 54
IT policy and procedure manual 54
Chapter 6: Performance measures 55
Critical success factors (CSFs) 55
Key performance indicators 56
Balanced scorecard 60
Metrics for customer satisfaction survey 60
Evaluation and appraisal 61
Quantitative evaluation 61
Qualitative evaluation 61
Chapter 7: An insight into the future 63
Current scenario 63
Future scenario 63
Key features 64
Objectives of a smart service desk 65
Role of the future service desk agent 66
Benefits to the organisation 66
ITIL 4 67
Chapter 8: Technology considerations 69
Artificial intelligence 69
Chatbots 70
Others uses of AI in the service desk 70
AI in IT support 70
Managers 72
AI in knowledge management 73
AI in change management 74
AI in IT asset management 74
Chapter 9: General reference 77

Contents

Tips for the service desk.. 77
Certifications for individuals...................................... 81
Certification for the service desk unit......................... 82
Common terms explained.. 83
Root cause analysis – overview.................................. 86
Root cause analysis methods...................................... 88
Chapter 10: Conclusion **93**
Further reading **95**

CHAPTER 1: WHAT IS A SERVICE DESK?

First and foremost, a service desk should be seen simply for what it is in the literal sense: a central location to go to when you need a service or someone to 'help' you with things.

It is your one-stop destination for enquiries, requests and reporting issues. It is your first touchpoint for any service offered by a service provider. A service desk adds structure to proceedings, whether it is as the front face for the internal customers or by allowing the technical support units to focus on the task at hand, without the continuous hassle of having to deal directly with internal customers.

Human interactions can vary, from the extremely pleasant to the utterly frustrating and demoralising. A service desk team almost completely bears the brunt of disgruntled customers, without allowing their grievances to reach any of the underlying support teams. This is a very important function that is often overlooked, as it is seen simply as part of a service desk agent's job and hence never appreciated enough.

You can have all the technical expertise and certifications in the world, but the ability to wake up each morning ready to 'go again' in a service desk environment is by far one of the most underrated skills in the corporate sphere. Ultimately, a good service desk is the glue that binds customers and service providers.

Mission and vision statements

It always helps to have a mission statement and a vision statement for the service desk. These serve as a constant reminder to each team member of their goals and responsibilities as well as those of the organisation. A sample is shown below, which can be altered as needed.

Mission:

To continually develop our services to meet and exceed customer expectations and contribute to the success of the organisation through the provision of timely, consistently high-quality and professional IT support at every customer contact, to assist all our customers in making the best use of technology in their business roles.

Vision:

To provide a customer-focused, single point of contact for IT services, taking ownership of issues and requests, making the best use of people and tools, and delivering useful, friendly support and advice to all customers.

The next section, though borne purely out of circumstantial observations, is worth at least a skim-through, as even seemingly small factors can have protracted effects on the overall well-being of the service desk agent.

The environment

As service desk agents spend their days communicating with customers, care should be taken to ensure that service desk teams are housed in an ***adequately spaced*** area, preferably secluded away from other teams, to avoid all the hustle and bustle of the office interfering with their conversations.

Having worked in an environment that was akin to sitting in an indoor ski resort, ***temperature settings*** maintained at an optimum can make a huge difference in creating an ideal working environment while also reducing the chances of agents falling sick.

As service desk agents are sedentary for the best part of their workday, choice of ***furniture***, not to be misinterpreted as expensive but that which makes long periods of sitting down comfortable, should be carefully considered. ***Headsets*** also play an important part in maintaining productivity levels.

Headsets

Picture a service desk agent in your mind and they will always be with wearing a headset. Although they serve as the perfect partner for every agent, headsets also come with a range of health hazards, especially if they are not used and maintained in the optimal manner. Some harmful effects are:

Bacterial infections

Headsets can stimulate bacterial growth in the ears, perhaps by increasing temperature and humidity levels within the auditory canal. This could be an issue for those who are prone to ear infections and thus more likely to have larger proportions of harmful bacteria in their ears.

Germs

The telephone, or the headset that accompanies it, can be one of the most prolific breeding grounds for germs in a workplace. Headsets should be cleaned regularly with a disinfectant to help reduce the build-up of disease-causing germs.

Hearing loss

The sound level of normal conversational speech is approximately 60 decibels, with 85 decibels generally considered the upper limit for safe listening. Although the likelihood of continuous exposure to harmful noise levels in a service desk environment is uncommon, the occasional break from a headset is always a good thing.

Vocal strain

Improper use of a headset can cause vocal strain, especially if the agent using the headset is talking throughout the day. Speaking in a quiet, relaxed manner helps to prevent vocal injuries.

Although individual staff might experience discomfort with a specific style of headset, this can easily be offset by making an alternative headset available. The remaining risks can be minimised through intelligent, proactive measures, such as the use of antibacterial wipes on earpieces and periodic replacement of their foam cushions. Setting mandatory volume limits and encouraging regular breaks reduces the likelihood of hearing loss.

The 50-minute rule

Agents should consider the 50-minute rule when it comes to working at the service desk. This basically means that they take a quick break every 50 minutes to stretch, drink water or maybe even meditate. The necessity and subsequent health benefits of following such a routine is often ignored, but it can have a long-term impact on the general well-being of an agent.

CHAPTER 2: PLANNING FOR A SERVICE DESK

There are a number of factors to consider when planning and setting up a service desk:

1. Type of support experience you want to deliver

In most cases, businesses will use their service desk in one of three ways:

- **Traditional or reactive** – responds to customer enquiries, fulfilling requests and resolving incidents as and when they are reported.
- **Holistic or proactive** – adapts to changing business needs by managing workflows, automating responses, centralising customer data and building a knowledge base, in addition to responding to customer enquiries.
- **Enterprise-wide customer service channel** – assists both external and internal customers, and acts as a central hub for proactive customer relationship management.

2. Staffing requirements

This will largely depend on the customer base, volume of enquiries anticipated to be handled via email and/or phone, and the operational hours expected to be covered.

To begin with, the expected utilisation rate of agents responding to customers can be set at approximately 70%.

The remaining 30% can be set aside for other activities such as breaks, meetings, training, etc. These figures must be reviewed periodically to ensure that customer wait times are not exceeding agreed levels or that agents are not experiencing extended 'idle' periods.

3. Well-defined categorisation and prioritisation

Tickets must be categorised, prioritised and assigned accurately to provide timely support based on levels agreed with the business.

4. Service level agreements (SLAs)

A well-documented SLA is a promise to customers that their issue will be responded to or resolved within a specified time frame. Multiple SLAs can be created with different response times depending on the type of ticket, product, customer group, or other defined criteria.

5. Knowledge base and self-service portal

Self-help content and a knowledge base of solutions for most common issues can be built through regular monitoring and trend analysis of tickets. Knowledge of these trends can be used to draft automated response templates, which save time.

Providing customers with a self-service portal also saves time, and demonstrates an understanding of their preferred workflows.

6. Track and improve on key metrics

Continuous improvement is vital to building a good reputation. This can be achieved through regular reviews of the organisation's key metrics as it helps to understand if the service provided is effective and also identify areas for improvements.

Likewise, qualitative feedback from customers, for example through customer satisfaction (CSAT) surveys, is invaluable to gaining insight into the health of the business. It also helps foster loyalty through positive customer support experiences.

CHAPTER 3: TELEPHONY AND ITSM TOOLS

The two important technological components of a service desk setup are telephony and the IT service management (ITSM) tool.

Telephony

Internet Protocol (IP), in simple terms, are a set of rules for routing and addressing data, sent as packets across networks, to ensure their arrival at the intended destination.

IP telephony is increasingly considered the preferred telephony solution, over a private branch exchange (PBX) system, due to the following benefits:

- Mobility and scalability – Unlike in a traditional phone system, there are no physical limitations while also providing the freedom to move as the business demands. Scalability is also hassle-free as more connections can be achieved by simply adding the number of licenses as per agents utilising this service.
- Lower installation and maintenance costs.
- Automatic call distribution.
- Computer telephony integration – when a customer contacts the service desk, their information will be visible to the agent, which will better prepare the agent to tackle the support issue. This eliminates the need to switch back and forth between programs to find information during a call.

- Easy integration with legacy systems and hardware.

Evaluation and selection

Selection of IP telephony vendors will boil down to the best value-for-money criteria with respect to features available and licensing methods of each.

Some of the basic features to be considered during selection include the following:

- Easy-to-use interface that provides a traditional telephony-like user experience.
- Security and reliability of voice and data traffic.
- Multi-language support.
- Full private branch exchange (PBX) features – which enable users within an organisation to communicate both internally and externally – including but not limited to caller ID, call forwarding, conference calling and voice messaging.
- Advanced call routing.
- User-friendly application installed on each agent's desktop for easier call handling.
- A supervisor module that includes live monitoring of agent activity.
- Ease of integration with the existing ITSM tool.

ITSM tool

ITSM can be defined as the set of activities that are performed by an organisation to design, plan, deliver, operate and control information technology (IT) services offered to customers.

To help ensure the widest adoption and maximise its effectiveness, the ITSM tool (service desk software) should be relatively easy to use, with a simple user interface that facilitates, rather than impedes, communication between an agent and customers.

Evaluation and selection

Some of the basic features to be considered during ITSM tool selection include the following:

- Integration with Active Directory – included in most Windows Server operating systems as a set of processes and services that stores information about objects on the company's network and makes this information easy for administrators and users to find and use.
- Multi-channel support so that customers can connect using the method of their choice – email, phone, ticket submission, live chat or social media.
- Telephony integration to quickly and easily retrieve customer information when you receive a call.
- Metrics, analytics and reporting to inform and optimise agents' performance and identify recurring trends.
- Self-service knowledge bases to make the most frequently requested information available to customers without the need of an agent.

- Routing tickets to the appropriate team or individual, whether based on skills or SLAs.
- Automatically monitoring ticket progress according to SLAs.
- Workflow integration between different modules in the ITSM tool.
- Licensing options, which can vary as per products and may follow any of the below methods:
  - o Subscription-based
  - o Perpetual
  - o Module-based
  - o User count

In addition, annual maintenance and support charges need to be considered before making the final decision.

ITSM configuration

Proper configuration of the ITSM tool is critical to ensuring that information captured is relevant and accurate. This includes, but is not limited to, the following:

- Add/import customer information.
- Add support groups and support personnel.
- Configure fields as mandatory (wherever appropriate).
- Configure classification (request, incident).
- Configure categorisation (categories and sub-categories).
- Configure prioritisation.

- Create templates for most common requests and incidents.
- Configure SLAs.
- Configure mail settings.
- Configure mail notifications.
- Customise email message templates.
- Configure short message service (SMS) notifications (if applicable).
- Add solutions to knowledge base.
- Configure reports and dashboards.
- Configure self-service portal.

CHAPTER 4: THE SERVICE DESK TEAM

Since service desk staff are the 'front face' of the IT department, it is of utmost importance to show the right attitude to the customer. The following are some of the core values, which should ideally form part of the team culture at a service desk, that must be incorporated into its day-to-day approach to service delivery:

Respect and integrity

Building and earning respect among each other and with customers and stakeholders, recognising each other's way of working and individual needs and requirements.

Teamwork

Combining skills and knowledge to deliver quality service to all customers and stakeholders. People are a service desk's greatest asset, and its strength and success depends on delivering together, as a unit.

Quality service and performance

Customer satisfaction is central to quality and performance. A service desk team must be committed to service excellence and must work to deliver a professional, proactive service to every customer. Each member of a service desk must strive to become an expert in their field and must be encouraged to regularly upgrade their skills to ensure continual improvement.

Efficient and proactive

It is imperative that every member of the service desk clearly understands the impact of service issues on the organisation it provides services to, and works with its customers, colleagues and stakeholders to prioritise requests effectively.

Single point of contact

Since the service desk is the single point of contact for all IT-related queries, service requests and communications, it must proactively communicate information relating to service delivery, including service availability, planned updates, and new and improved procedures through a variety of methods, such as face to face, telephone and email.

The service desk agent

A job as a service desk agent is often seen by many as an entry point and training ground within organisations for those with little or no previous experience. However, there are a range of soft skills to look for in candidates to determine whether they would be a good fit.

Figure 1: Service agent qualities

Though it might not be possible to tick all the boxes, anyone with the majority of the below qualities, in no particular order, will prove a key asset to a service desk team.

- A good listener.
- Polite and empathetic, with a strong desire to help people.
- Patient and calm.
- Service-oriented.
- Excellent communication skills.
- Organised, with documentation skills.
- Quick learner with a keen eye for detail.
- Ability to multitask while maintaining focus for long periods.

- Flexible and responds to change in a positive manner.
- Critical thinking and problem-solving abilities.
- Sense of urgency – will act promptly, decisively and without delay.
- Team player with top interpersonal skills.
- Are able to deal with other people's low levels of appreciation of them and value of their role (from customers or colleagues, it is a thankless job after all).
- A technical background. Although not essential, this gives an edge over other candidates.

In addition to the inherent qualities mentioned, agents also need to be provided with relevant awareness sessions and training programmes to ensure high-quality services are provided to their customers. Every organisation needs to have this at the top of its list of priorities.

From personal experience, such training often overlooks the organisation's business goals and objectives, which can contribute to a disconnection between customers and the service desk (and, at times, IT in general) during the assessment and subsequent prioritisation of incidents. A central repository of service-related documentation such as, standard operating procedure, list of critical business systems, service level agreements, prioritisation matrix, etc. should be made available to the service desk to alleviate this concern.

Responsibilities of a service desk agent

Some generic job responsibilities of a service desk agent are listed below:

- Follow standard service desk operating procedures and accurately log all incoming cases, via telephone and/or email, using the service desk software, ensuring courteous, timely and effective delivery of first-line support of customer issues.
- Ensure high availability to customers by maintaining a high call-handling rate via the telephony system.
- Identify, evaluate and prioritise customer requests and issues.
- Actively identify, assess, record, resolve and/or escalate incidents and service requests, ensuring they are handled within an agreed time limit, within agreed processes and in a professional and customer-sensitive manner.
- Troubleshoot basic customer issues and provide basic desktop support.
- Proactively follow-up of all cases reported from start through to a successful resolution, ensuring that all cases are resolved within the agreed SLA.
- Prepare various service desk-related reports and communicate the same to management and relevant support teams, as and when required.
- Participate in a shift-based roster, whenever applicable.

The service desk manager

Next, we take a look at some of the responsibilities of a service desk manager, which may vary depending on the size of the organisation. In some organisations, the service desk manager performs the role of incident or problem manager in addition to their daily role at the service desk.

Responsibilities of a service desk manager:

- Manage and mentor the service desk team.
- Monitor incident and service request dashboards to ensure adherence to the SLA.
- Ownership of the service request fulfilment process to ensure all requests are routed through to the appropriate teams and completed within the agreed SLA.
- Ownership of the incident management process to ensure minimal impact of incidents upon service quality.
- Develop and maintain a standard operating procedure (SOP) manual, internal process documents and relevant forms for successful running of daily service desk operations.
- Define key performance indicators (KPIs) and objectives for the service desk team and ensure consistent performance to meet or exceed these KPIs.
- Prepare statistical and management reports, analyse trends and identify improvement opportunities.
- Perform CSAT surveys, and develop action plans to address areas needing improvement.
- Develop and maintain operational level agreements (OLAs) with various support groups.

Wherever appropriate, the following responsibilities can be added to those above.

- Ownership of the problem management process to ensure minimal impact of incidents upon service quality.
- Prepare responses and formulate action plans to address all points raised during audits and risk assessments related to the service desk.

CHAPTER 5: DOCUMENTATION

A centralised repository, with appropriate access provided to the manager and agents, is a must for storing documents related to the daily operational tasks of the service desk.

Some of the documents in use at a service desk are detailed below.

Standard operating procedure manual (SOP)

An SOP manual must be designed with the purpose of serving as a quick reference guide for members of the service desk for performing their daily operational tasks. Though the contents of an SOP manual will vary depending on the organisation, the following gives a general idea/overview of the sections that may be included:

- **Introduction:**
  - Mission
  - Vision
  - Purpose
  - Scope
- **Process overview:**
  - Objectives
  - Process owner
  - Stakeholders
- **Process details:**
  - Operating hours
  - Responsibilities of a service desk agent

- o List of tasks performed by a service desk agent
- o Incident and service request logging procedures – flowcharts
- o Call handling procedure
- o Email management procedure
- o List of systems and applications used by the service desk
- o Key performance measures (KPMs) and KPIs
- o Details of reports and dashboards (operational and management)
- o RACI matrix
- **List of acronyms used**
- **Glossary of terms used (ITIL® definitions, if applicable)**
- **Appendices – display links to documents such as:**
  - o Solution database
  - o SLAs
  - o Prioritisation matrix
  - o IT escalation matrix
  - o Service request matrix
  - o Forms
  - o Other relevant documents stored in a centralised repository

Knowledge base (solution database)

A knowledge base is essentially a central repository of solutions for IT support staff and customers. It has become a critical component of service delivery as it gives customers the chance to solve their problems without contacting the service desk.

A knowledge base is no longer considered a nice-to-have add-on, but is what customers, displaying an increasing preference for self-service over human interaction, expect as a basic support feature.

At the service provider end, this can reduce calls to the service desk as well as overall support costs, and ensure consistency in the support delivered.

Solutions that are uploaded to a knowledge base will cover the following:

- First-level support.
- Second-level support.
- Known errors and workarounds.

Process documents

In this section we will discuss, in brief, the processes and related documentation that require service desk involvement. Though these are more prevalent in organisations that have implemented the information technology infrastructure library (ITIL) framework, there are tangible benefits for any organisation that chooses to adopt them, even if it has not implemented ITIL.[1]

---

[1] For more information about ITIL, see chapter 7.

Request fulfilment

The request fulfilment process is responsible for managing the lifecycle of all service requests submitted by customers either by contacting the service desk directly or through a service catalogue. A service catalogue can be defined as an organised and accurate collection of information on all IT services offered by an organisation's IT department.

The corresponding process document created may include, but is not limited to, the following components:

- **Introduction/overview:**
  o Purpose
  o Scope
  o Objectives
  o Process owner
  o Stakeholders
- **Process details:**
  o Request types
  o SLA details
  o Tooling details and user guide (included in the appendix)
  o Stages of the request lifecycle:
    - Request for service
    - Logging and validation
    - Categorisation and prioritisation
    - Request review and authorisation
    - Request fulfilment and closure
  o Roles and responsibilities:
    - Level 1 support

- Level 2 support
- Other stakeholders who provide input into the request fulfilment process
○ Request fulfilment flowchart:
  - Level 1
○ KPIs
○ RACI matrix – A RACI matrix (also called a responsibility assignment matrix or linear responsibility chart), describes the participation by various roles in completing tasks or deliverables for an existing process. It is an acronym that stands for "Responsible, Accountable, Consulted and Informed". Each role that is a stakeholder in a process will fall under one of these.

- **Appendix:**
  ○ Glossary of terms (ITIL® definitions, if applicable)
  ○ Reference to supporting documents

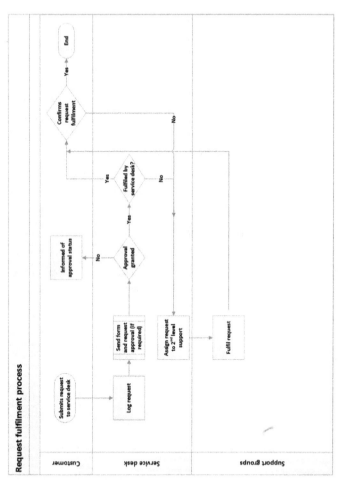

Figure 2: Request fulfilment process

Incident management

The incident management process document specifies in detail the various steps in an incident lifecycle. This document may include, but is not limited to, the following components:

- **Introduction/overview:**
  - ○ Purpose
  - ○ Scope
  - ○ Objectives
  - ○ Process owner
  - ○ Stakeholders
- **Process details:**
  - ○ SLA details (priority vs resolution)
  - ○ Tooling details and user guide (included in appendix)
  - ○ Stages of incident lifecycle:
    - - Detect and log
    - - Classify and prioritise
    - - Investigation and diagnosis
    - - Resolution and recovery
    - - Review and closure
  - ○ Roles and responsibilities:
    - - Level 1 support
    - - Level 2 support
    - - Level 3 support (vendors)
    - - Other stakeholders who provide input into the incident management process

- o Incident management flowcharts:
  - Level 1
  - Level 2
- o Support groups matrix
- o Incident prioritisation matrix
- o Service level targets:
  - Level 1 support (phone, email response)
  - Time to resolve as a % (priority-wise)
- o KPIs
- o Business continuity plan
- o RACI matrix
- **Appendix:**
  - o Glossary of terms (ITIL definitions, if applicable)
  - o Reference to supporting documents

Responsibilities of an incident manager

- Point of contact for all major incidents.
- Develop and maintain incident management process and procedures.
- Responsible for planning and coordinating all the activities required to perform, monitor and report on the incident management process.
- Monitor the incidents to ensure that the SLAs are adhered to.
- Identify, initiate, schedule and conduct incident reviews.

- Establish continuous process improvement cycles where the process performance, activities, roles and responsibilities, policies, procedures and supporting technology is reviewed and enhanced where applicable.

RACI matrix

Table 1 lists out the various actions that form part of the incident management process, the various stakeholders involved (from detection to post-resolution activities) and their level of responsibility (**R**esponsible, **A**ccountable, **C**onsulted, **I**nformed).

Table 1: RACI Matrix for an Incident Management Process

Action	Customers	Service desk	Level 2 support	Level 3 support – vendors	Incident manager	IT management
Detect incident	A	C, I				
Record incident	C	A, R				
Record symptoms	C	A, R				

Action	Customers	Service desk	Level 2 support	Level 3 support – vendors	Incident manager	IT management
Classify incident	I	A, R				
Communicate known errors	I	A, R				
Communicate solutions	C, I	A, R				
Relate incidents to parent cases		A, R			I	
Prioritise incident	I	R	R		A, I	
Major incident assignment		A, R			C	I
Communicate major incident		A, R	I		I	I
Second line support assignment	I	A, R	I		I	

Action	Customers	Service desk	Level 2 support	Level 3 support – vendors	Incident manager	IT management
Vendor assignment			A, R	I	I	
Defect assignment			A, R	I, C		
Investigation and diagnosis	C	A, R	A, R	R		
Incident resolution		R	A, R	R	A	
Incident closure	I	R	R		A	
Monitoring		R			A	C, I
Reporting					A	C, I
Problem identification			R		A	C, I
Create solutions		I	R, A		I	
Update known errors		I	R		A	

Action	Customers	Service desk	Level 2 support	Level 3 support – vendors	Incident manager	IT management
Provision of code fixes			A, R	A		
Vendor SLA management			A, R	C, I	I	I
Incident process development		I	I		A, R	C, I

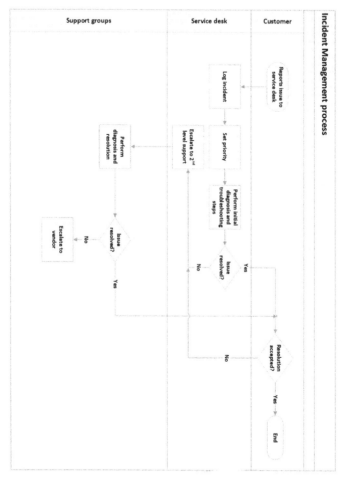

Figure 3: Incident management process

Figure 3 shows a diagrammatic explanation of the incident management process as described in earlier sections. The activities that form part of this process and the various stakeholders involved in these activities help define responsibilities clearly and without any ambiguity.

Major incident management

The major incident management process document specifies in detail the various steps involved in a major incident lifecycle. This document may include, but is not limited to, the following components:

- **Introduction/overview:**
  o Purpose
  o Scope
  o Objectives
  o Process owner
  o Stakeholders
- **Process details:**
  o Stages of major incident lifecycle:
    - Engage major incident manager
    - Management escalation and notification via phone and email
    - Review impact of incident reported
    - Establish a major incident team
    - Open a major incident report
    - Analyse incident
    - Perform risk assessment
    - Communication of plan

- Implement resolution plan
- Confirm status
- Closing communication
- Resolve incident in tooling system

o KPIs
o Post-incident review
o Escalation matrix
o RACI matrix

- **Appendix:**
  o Reference to supporting documents

RACI matrix

Table 2 lists out the various actions that form part of the major incident management process, the various stakeholders involved (from detection to post-resolution activities) and their level of responsibility (**R**esponsible, **A**ccountable, **C**onsulted, **I**nformed).

Table 2: RACI Matrix for a Major Incident Management Process

Action	Customers	Service desk	Level 2 support	Level 3 / vendor	Incident manager	Major incident manager (MIM)	IT management	Business	Information security office (ISO)
Detect incident	A	A, I							
Record incident	C	A, R							
Record symptoms	C	A, R							
Classify incident	I	A, R							
Communicate known errors	I	A, R							
Communicate solutions	C, I	A, R							
Relate incidents to		A, R			I	I			

Action	Customers	Service desk	Level 2 support	Level 3 / vendor	Incident manager	Major incident manager (MIM)	IT management	Business	Information security office (ISO)
parent cases									
Prior-itise incident	I	R	R		C, I	A, I			
Major incident assign-ment		A, R			C	I			
Review major incident	C	C	C			A, R			
Comm-unicate major incident		R			I	A	I	I	
Second-line support assign-ment	I	A, R	I			A, R			

Action	Customers	Service desk	Level 2 support	Level 3 / vendor	Incident manager	Major incident manager (MIM)	IT management	Business	Information security office (ISO)
Vendor assignment		I	A, R	I	I	I	I	I	
Defect assignment		I	A, R	I, C	I	I	I	I	
Investigation	C	I	A, R	A, R	I	I	I	I	
Incident diagnosis	C	I	A, R	A, R	I	I	I	I	C
Incident resolution	I	I	A, R	A, R	I	A	I	I	C
Incident closure	I	C, I	I		I	A, R	I	I	
Monitoring	C	A, R			I	R			
Reporting		C	C		A, R		I		

Action	Customers	Service desk	Level 2 support	Level 3 / vendor	Incident manager	Major incident manager (MIM)	IT management	Business	Information security office (ISO)
Problem identi-fication		I	R, C	R, C	A	C			
Create solu-tions		I	A, R	A, R	I				
Update known errors		I	R		A				
Provi-sion of code fixes			R	A	I				
Creation of major incident report					R	A, R			
MIM process develop-ment		I			C, R	C, I	I		

Problem management

The problem management process document details the processes and guidelines related to the lifecycle of a problem record. This document may include, but is not limited to, the following components:

- **Introduction/overview:**
  - Purpose
  - Scope
  - Objectives
  - Process owner
  - Stakeholders
- **Process details:**
  - Stages of a problem lifecycle:
    - Log and review
    - Prioritise and assign
    - Diagnose and solve
    - Monitor and resolve
    - Review and close
  - Workflow diagram
  - Roles and responsibilities of various stakeholders:
    - Problem manager
    - IT support groups
    - Other stakeholders who provide input into problem management process
  - Problem prioritisation matrix:

- o Overview of root cause analysis (RCA) method used[2]
- o KPIs
- o Service level targets:
    - Completion of RCA (based on priority of incident)
    - Problem resolution
- **Appendix:**
    - o Reference to supporting documents

Responsibilities of a problem manager

- Responsible for managing the lifecycle of all problem records, ensuring that these are diagnosed, logged and escalated to appropriate and consistent quality standards.
- Develop and maintain known error database and workarounds.
- Ensures RCA sessions are conducted in a timely manner.
- Ensure all actions identified and agreed during RCA sessions and are completed as per agreed SLAs.
- Ensures reactive and proactive management of IT issues and known errors.
- Closes all problem records.

---

[2] For more information about RCA, see chapter 9.

RACI matrix

Table 3 lists out the various actions that form part of the problem management process, the various stakeholders involved (from detection to post-closure activities) and their level of responsibility (**R**esponsible, **A**ccountable, **C**onsulted, **I**nformed).

Table 3: RACI Matrix for a Problem Management Process

Activity	Problem manager	RCA lead	Change coordinator
Problem detection, logging and categorisation	A, R	I	
Problem investigation and diagnosis	A	R	
Problem resolution	A	R	R
Create known error record	A	R	
Document workaround solution	A	R	
Problem review and closure	A, R		
Problem monitoring	A, R		

Update knowledge base with workaround solution	A	R	

Incident prioritisation matrix

An incident's priority can be determined by assessing its urgency and impact. 'Urgency' is a measure of how quickly the incident needs to be resolved whereas 'impact' is a measure of the extent and/or potential damage caused by the incident before it can be resolved.

Each organisation may adopt its own method of prioritising incidents.

One approach may be to develop a priority matrix depending on the following:

- Number of external customers impacted.
- Number of internal customers (end users) impacted.
- Financial impact.
- Impact of the incident on the organisation's reputation.
- Availability of a workaround to reduce impact of the incident.

Table 4 is a sample of an incident priority matrix using the above criteria:

Table 4: Sample of an Incident Priority Matrix

Category	Description
Critical (P1)	• A large number of external customers are affected. • A large number of internal customers (end users) are affected. • Significant financial impact likely to exceed <*amount*>. • Significant impact to the reputation of the business.
High (P2)	• A moderate number of external customers are affected. • A moderate number of internal customers (end users) are affected. • Considerable financial impact likely to exceed <*amount*> but not more than <*amount*>. • Considerable impact to the reputation of the business.
Medium (P3)	• A minimal number of external customers are affected and/or have access to an acceptable level of service through a workaround. A minimal number of internal customers (end users) are affected and/or inconvenienced but not in a significant way.

Category	Description
	• Minimal financial impact, likely to be less than *<amount>*. • Minimal damage to the reputation of the business.
Low (P4)	• Single internal customer (end user) is affected. • No external customers impacted. • No financial impact. • No impact on reputation.

An alternative approach may be to develop a priority matrix based on the criticality of the organisation's infrastructure and applications being managed with respect to business outcomes and the related services being provided to internal and external customers.

Incident escalation matrix

This is primarily used during the major incident management processes to keep all key IT and business stakeholders informed on the progress of the incident and may contain the following:

- Name
- Title
- Contact number(s)
- Elapsed time before contact (based on priority – P1/P2)

Problem prioritisation matrix

The priority of a problem record may be determined by taking the following factors into consideration:

- Criticality of infrastructure and applications impacted.
- Probability of incident recurrence.
- Financial impact.
- Availability of workaround to reduce impact of the related incident.

Note: SLAs for completion of each action agreed towards problem resolution must be determined based on the priority of the problem record.

Operational level agreement (OLA)

An OLA defines the relationships between the service provider's support groups, in support of an SLA.

The agreement describes the responsibilities of each internal support group toward other support groups, including the process and time frame for delivery of its services.

The various points that need to be covered while drafting an OLA include, but are not limited to, the following:

- **Introduction/overview:**
  - Purpose
  - Scope
  - Objectives
  - Parties involved
  - Duration

- **Details of agreement:**
  - o List of services provided
  - o List of tasks under each service
  - o Escalation matrix – helps define multiple layers of support personnel to be notified during the lifecycle of an incident and escalation procedures during critical issues.
  - o Contact mechanism
  - o Service review plan – aims to **review** business and infrastructure **services** on a regular basis to improve **service** quality, and where necessary to identify more economical ways of providing a **service**.

Service catalogue

A service catalogue is a database or structured document with information about all live IT services, including those available for deployment. An organisations can implement a service catalogue in several ways, ranging from a simple but structured Excel spreadsheet, to customised databases, to the use of their existing ITSM tool.

Below are the basic steps to start building a service catalogue:

- Collect information about business units and services.
- Determine what is important to define a service.
- Determine dependencies.

The amount of information within a service catalogue will differ from organisations as well as the availability of dedicated individuals to perform each role.

Table 5 provides an example of the information to be collected about an IT service. Similar information of all services being provided will be put together to form the service catalogue.

Table 5: Example of a Service Template

Service name	The agreed name for the service.
Service description	A brief description of what the service does, and the expected outcomes.
Service category	Classify the service into one of the categories previously agreed. Categories are important to provide the service catalogue with a hierarchical view of services.
Business unit(s)	Business unit(s) to which the service is provided.
Business impact	Describe the positive impact of having the service available and/or the negative impact of the opposite. The impact can be quantified by the number of customers affected, the impact on each customer, and the cost to the business.

Business contacts	Name and contact information of the key business person(s) to be contacted.
Service level agreement (SLA)	It is usually better to provide a link to the document with the SLA encompassing the IT service.
Service hours	Write here the agreed time period when the IT service should be available.
Service owner(s)	Name and contact information of the person(s) with this role.
Escalation contacts	Name and contact information of the person(s) to be contacted when an escalation procedure is triggered.
Service reports	A list of the operational reports available for the IT service.
Service reviews	Frequency of the service level review meetings.
Request procedures	Describe how the service should be requested.
Policies	Describe any policies governing the use of the service.
Supporting services	List any supporting services on which the IT service depends.

Services supported	List any services this service is supporting.

Service request approval matrix

A well-defined approval matrix for handling service requests facilitates accurate and quick handling of customer requests and also removes ambiguity at the service desk on authorisation levels and veto (override) rights of approvers.

IT policy and procedure manual

This document provides the policies and procedures for selection and use of IT within the organisation that must be followed by all staff. It also provides guidelines to administer these policies, with the correct procedure to follow.

CHAPTER 6: PERFORMANCE MEASURES

The overall performance of a service desk can be evaluated through an analysis of its critical success factors (CSFs) and KPIs. Metrics must be set against agreed targets and then measured and reported to ensure they are being met or whether improvement plans need to be put in place.

Critical success factors (CSFs)

At the highest level of a measurement system are the CSFs. CSFs need to be met to achieve your goals, and can span process, people, product, partner and performance.

Service desk CSFs may include:

- **Organisations and people** – Agents have adequate competency and knowledge of the IT services, technology and organisations they support, as well as being a part of a culture that supports the organisation's objectives.
- **Value streams and processes** – Agents work in an integrated and coordinated way with customers and an internal support unit to enable value creation.
- **Information and technology** – The ticketing system includes workflows to enable appropriate ticket management and escalation procedures.
- **Partners and suppliers** – SLAs and OLAs exist for external and internal service providers (technical and application infrastructure areas) respectively.

- **Performance** – Service desk staff are aware of KPIs for their roles.

Key performance indicators

KPIs are a measure of performance that enable organisations to obtain information about effectiveness and efficiency of their processes and operations.

Below are some common examples of KPIs to measure service desk performance. Targets for each must be set in agreement with relevant IT and business stakeholders.

**Table 6: Common examples of KPIs for
Service Desk Performance**

KPI	Description
Agent availability	Number of hours that an agent is logged in to the telephony system.
Time per call	Average time taken by an agent to handle customer enquiries, requests or issues.
Call pick-up rate	Percentage of calls answered within a specific time (for example, less than 15 seconds, less than 30 seconds, etc.).
Abandoned call rate	Percentage of calls abandoned by customers

KPI	Description
	while waiting to be answered by a service desk agent.
Customer hold time rate	Percentage of calls where the customer is put on hold for a specific time while waiting for a response (for example, 90 seconds, 180 seconds, etc.).
Average time for completion of service requests	Number of hours taken to complete service requests.
Service request completed within SLA	Percentage of service requests completed within the SLA.
Rate of first-line incident resolution	Percentage of incidents resolved by the service desk.
Incidents within SLA	Percentage of incidents resolved within the SLA.
Incorrect ticket assignment	Percentage of tickets that were incorrectly assigned.
Repeat incidents	Number of incidents reported to be recurring.

KPI	Description
Reactivated incidents	Percentage of incidents reactivated/reopened by the customer.
Customer satisfaction (CSAT) rate	Overall percentage of customer satisfaction with the service desk.

In addition to the above, the below metrics can also be measured at the service desk, pertaining to second- and third-level support.

Table 7: Common Examples of KPIs for Second and Third Level Support

KPI	Description
Average time for completion of service requests	Number of hours taken to complete service requests.
Service request completed within SLA	Percentage of service requests completed within the SLA.
Average resolution time for P1 incidents	Average time taken to resolve P1 incidents.
Average resolution time for P2 incidents	Average time taken to resolve P2 incidents.

KPI	Description
Average resolution time for P3 incidents	Average time taken to resolve P3 incidents.
Average resolution time for P4 incidents	Average time taken to resolve P4 incidents.
P1 incidents resolved within SLA	Percentage of P1 incidents resolved within the SLA.
P2 incidents resolved within SLA	Percentage of P2 incidents resolved within the SLA.
P3 incidents resolved within SLA	Percentage of P3 incidents resolved within the SLA.
P4 incidents resolved within SLA	Percentage of P4 incidents resolved within the SLA.
Reassigned incidents	Number of tickets that were reassigned between individuals within a support group.
Repeat incidents	Number of incidents reported to be recurring.
Reactivated incidents	Percentage of incidents reactivated/reopened by customers.

KPI	Description
Maintain quality of IT services	Number and percentage of major incidents reported against each IT service.

Balanced scorecard

A balanced scorecard (BSC) serves the purpose of aligning the IT department with the business, so that its metrics can be tracked alongside enterprise-wide metrics. A BSC helps build IT value in the organisation and also helps in long-term objectives like automation and reallocation of existing resources into newer projects wherever applicable.

While preparing and publishing the BSC report is not a responsibility of the service desk, many of the metrics measured at the service desk form part of the 'operational excellence' quadrant of a BSC.

Metrics for customer satisfaction survey

Below are a few common metrics that can be used in surveys to evaluate CSAT levels with the service desk.

- Professionalism.
- Communication skills.
- Mechanism for reporting issues.
- Accessibility and availability.
- Willingness to take ownership of reported issues.
- Ability to solve reported issues quickly and accurately.
- Understanding of business objectives.

- Reliable service.
- Relationship with business units.
- Eagerness to help.

These can be scored on a scale of 1–5, with 1 denoting 'very dissatisfied' and 5 denoting 'extremely satisfied'.

Evaluation and appraisal

The annual evaluation and appraisal process for service desk agents can be categorised into quantitative and qualitative measures.

Quantitative evaluation

The metrics used for quantitative evaluation of an agent will include those mentioned under KPIs, for example:

- Agent availability.
- Time per call.
- Call pick-up rate.
- Abandoned call rate.
- Customer hold-time rate.
- Average time for completion of service requests.
- Service request completed within SLA.
- Rate of first-line incident resolution.

Qualitative evaluation

This category can help assess an agent's contribution to the overall image of the service desk team, which is just as vital as quantitative achievements. Common metric include:

6: Performance measures

- Respond effectively to assigned responsibilities.
- Meet attendance requirement.
- Honour commitment and attitude towards work.
- Interpersonal skills.
- Responsiveness to change.

CHAPTER 7: AN INSIGHT INTO THE FUTURE

Current scenario

Service desks in a lot of organisations are in a legacy mode where support mechanism for customers are provided through the use of:

- Self-service portal;
- Service catalogue;
- Service desk software; and
- Telephony support.

While this might be the most cost-effective option for small and medium-sized businesses, there are a few disadvantages:

- Low rate of incident reduction.
- Limited means of communication (phone, email).
- Insufficient information of customer.
- CSAT ratings lower than anticipated due to customer experience not reaching the required levels.
- Agent to customer community ratio increases as per increase in business expectations.

Future scenario

More and more organisations are using technological advancements and moving towards a 'smarter' version of the service desk, by adopting intelligent and predictive analysis to achieve this.

The figure below demonstrates the benefits that can be derived through this method.

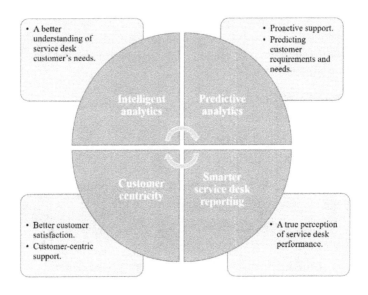

Figure 4: Benefits of a 'smart' service desk

Key features

Some features that come with moving to a smart service desk:

- Use of **service intelligence** (cognitive analytics, big data analytics) to aggregate available data of customers. This is used to *'personalise' customer experience*, which includes determining the 'IT skill level' of customers to enable agents to respond accordingly.

- Integration of a **virtual agent** into the service desk self-service portal, which *acts as a personal assistant for every individual customer's business needs*. For example, this can be used to fill in timesheets on a phone or to fix an IT issue.

- An **inter-connected omni-channel** to make sure *customers do not have to repeat their issues* to different levels of support *during call hand-off*.

- Use of **voice biometrics** that *enables customers to authenticate themselves* before they talk to an agent.

- **Intelligent automation** to *increase efficiency* and *reduce costs* using autonomics and cognitive platforms.

- **Predictive analysis** to *enable customer issues* to be *detected* and addressed *before they cause problems*.

- **Channelling customers** shift-left **towards self-service** is the way to *achieve cost reduction*. This is perhaps the most important factor to customers.

Objectives of a smart service desk

- **Greater user experience (UX)** through easy-to-use consistent user interface (single intelligent system).

- **Eliminate the need to interact with multiple applications** for daily core tasks through an intelligent virtual agent.

- **Have information about customers ready at hand** when they connect to an agent using artificial intelligence (AI).
- **Improve utilisation of service desk agents** by eliminating execution of low-level tasks through automation.
- **Build, categorise and maintain knowledge** for support purposes (chatbots) with the help of methods such as machine learning (ML) and natural language processing.
- **Make informed, rational decisions** on behalf of customers using cognitive analysis.

Role of the future service desk agent

When the objectives listed above are met, future service desk agents will be able to move from repetitive manual tasks to higher skilled tasks such as:

- Overseeing machine-enabled support;
- Interpreting data analysis about customers;
- Resolving issues ahead of time or in real time;
- Providing personalised support to customers; and
- Identifying opportunities for using new/emerging technologies.

Benefits to the organisation

Planning and implementing a smart service desk will provide the following benefits to the organisation:

- The implied efficiency of an automated system that learns dynamically should significantly reduce the total cost of ownership (TCO) of support.
- Biometrics such as voice recognition and voice identification will add a layer of security and speed up the resolution of issues, helping the chief experience officer (CxO) or other C-suite executives secure company data, while facilitating the concept of 'anytime, anywhere' to ensure high availability of service provision to end users.
- By consumerisation of business support in this way, the CxO will enhance the user experience of the organisation's workers.
- Apps and environments will self-provision based on the preferences and choices of the individual, leading to content and efficient employees.

ITIL 4

ITIL (information technology infrastructure library), is a set of detailed practices for IT service management that focuses on aligning IT services with the needs of business. It describes the various processes and procedures that can be applied by an organisation to enhance their strategy, value of delivery, and help them establish a baseline from which the organisation can plan, implement, and measure services as well as measure their improvement.

ITIL has gone through several revisions and the most recent version is ITIL 4.

ITIL 4 puts service management in a strategic context, looks at ITSM, development, operations, business relationships and governance holistically and brings the different functions together. By doing this, ITIL 4 has evolved into an integrated model for digital service management. It enables IT professionals to support their organisation on its journey to digital transformation and support world-class digital services by incorporating all the best things from ITIL.

The key elements of ITIL 4 are the *four dimensions*, the *7 guiding principles*, the move from processes to *practices*, and the *Service Value System*, providing a holistic approach to the *co-creation of value* through service relationships.

I will not delve into the details of each element since that is not in the scope of this book. However, for those interested in learning more about ITIL 4, I strongly recommend *ITIL*® *4 Essentials – Your essential guide for the ITIL 4 Foundation exam and beyond, second edition* by Claire Agutter.[3]

---

[3] *www.itgovernancepublishing.co.uk/product/itil-4-essentials-your-essential-guide-for-the-itil-4-foundation-exam-and-beyond-second-edition*.

CHAPTER 8: TECHNOLOGY CONSIDERATIONS

In this chapter, we take a look at AI, how it can be used to progress towards a smart service desk, and its applications in various areas.

Artificial intelligence

The impact of AI on existing service desks can fall into one of three categories:

1. **Smart automation – using chatbots**
   - Categorising, prioritising and assigning tickets.
   - Handling level 1 incidents with documented resolutions.
2. **Strategic insights**
   - Finding the right window for pushing patches to large number of machines.
   - Performing impact analysis to aid in change planning, implementation and review.
3. **Predictive analysis**
   - Flagging reports that could violate the SLA.
   - Identifying potential IT problems and change failure patterns.

Chatbots

A chatbot is an application that interacts with customers, using a conversational platform. AI, machine learning (ML) and natural language processing are used in the development of a chatbot.

Chatbots engage in real-time human-like conversations to make everyday jobs simpler, easier and more efficient, and also improve productivity by handling repetitive service desk tasks such as classification and categorisation of tickets, responding to end users for frequently asked questions (FAQs), etc. much faster.

Others uses of AI in the service desk

- Automating the employee onboarding process.
- ML-based models can recognise patterns in the historic employee onboarding requests database to suggest what hardware and software should be delivered at the time of request creation.
- ML-based models can also analyse the types of requests created by new employees a few months into their job and use this during the onboarding process to avoid multiple requests being created.

AI in IT support

AI-driven automation allows all levels of IT support to more effectively share and access valuable information, allowing them to better align their support functions with the needs and expectations of customers.

As a result, IT organisations can move from a reactive to proactive posture in terms of delivering and supporting business objectives.

Level 1 – benefits to the service desk:

- Auto-populate data (such as employee ID, assigned assets, contact information and related incidents) from multiple systems into incident records.
- Gain access to related information commonly reserved for level 2 staff (such as configuration management database (CMDB) access and application/system configuration details).
- Provide real-time suggestions to requests based on issue type and location, allowing quick resolution, order goods and services, via self-service.
- Spend less time on repetitive tasks and more time on RCA of issues, helping to minimise escalations, reduce mean time to repair (MTTR), and reduce future incidents.

Level 2 – benefits to second level support

- Automatically categorise, prioritise and assign incidents to specific support agents based on the request's specific issue type, location, etc.
- Populate incident records with valuable information such as related incidents, configuration items, system changes and known issues/resolutions.

- Gain real-time and predictive insights into incident trends to limit unnecessary downtime and ensure SLAs are maintained.
- Spend less time performing RCA of common issues and focus more on strategic initiatives, such as new operating system rollouts, and device and application deployments.

Level 3 – benefits to third level support or vendor

- Gain visibility into incidents and trends regarding service disruptions associated with new systems and service rollouts, non-tested applications and infrastructure failures.
- Surface and correlate IT and business data to optimise systems while reducing the footprint of services experiencing little to no usage.
- Dedicate more time to preventive maintenance, research and innovation.
- Reduces the need for level 3 involvement by empowering self-service through level 2 to perform tasks previously reserved for level 3.

Managers

Implementation of AI and various support levels as explained in the earlier section will in turn result in freeing up the respective managers to perform more meaningful tasks, with AI at the heart of these. Some of these tasks are as listed below:

- Surface operational data in real time to measure the health of IT services by topic, geography, team and role.
- Proactively assess future resource requirements, vendor relationships and budget requirements by correlating and displaying valuable IT and business data.
- Use trend analytics insights regarding the adoption of employee self-service, support costs and CSAT scores.

AI in knowledge management

The benefits of using AI in knowledge management are:

- Specific ML-based models can be trained to identify the success rate for each solution in a knowledge base on historic performance.
- Based on metrics, an ML-based model can suggest which articles should be retired and which could be improved.
- The grading of solutions based on their performance over time will assist chatbots during a chat session.
- An ML model can flag these categories based on the severity of the above parameters. It can also deliver insight into which categories need more knowledge management efforts.

AI in change management

AI can learn from the available history of IT change records and offer the service desk a variety of insights and suggestions at different points in change workflows, such as:

- **Planning** – The right window to implement changes of a particular category or on a particular configuration item.
- **Risk evaluation** – The cascading impact of issues.
- **Evaluation by the change advisory board (CAB)** – Critical failure points and areas of conflicts in the change workflow.
- **Implementation** – Signs of change failure and proactive warnings to initiate change rollback.

AI in IT asset management

The benefits of using AI in IT asset management are:

- ML systems can constantly monitor the performance of a configuration item and predict breakdowns, thus assisting service desk teams monitor and manage IT hardware and software assets better.
- AI can help service desk tools flag anomalies and generate critical warnings by connecting the dots across multiple areas.

Platforms and tools

Common platforms and tools used to implement AI:

- Microsoft® Azure
- Microsoft Cognitive Toolkit (previously known as CNTK)
- Google AI tools (e.g. TensorFlow)
- IBM Watson
- Moogsoft® AIOps
- Blue Prism®
- UiPath™

CHAPTER 9: GENERAL REFERENCE

Tips for the service desk

Below are a few tips that every service desk team should follow to provide a world-class experience to its customers.

Tip 1: Be easy to reach

Accessibility and availability are two key factors to the successful running of a service desk. Some customers will want to call the service desk, some will want to log everything in an email or online via a self-service portal, and some will prefer to do it via social media or an online chat.

So, make it easy for them to engage with your service desk by providing a number of channels through which they can get in touch.

Tip 2: Make your customer experience consistent

Whether a customer gets through to an experienced service desk agent or a brand-new one, the experience should be the same – and this means consistent as well as excellent!

As mentioned at the beginning of this book, training and standards are important, but common sense also plays a big part.

Tip 3: Respond to all contacts, and keep them updated

A lot of service desk traffic is actually generated by customers having to call/email again to either check that their ticket is progressing or hasn't been lost forever in the black hole of IT support. Responding in a professional way reassures the customer and sets a positive tone for their next interaction with IT.

Tip 4: Write good call notes

"Empty" or incomplete incident records are harmful to service desks. Make sure that incident records are updated regularly and shared with customers when appropriate so that:

- The customer will understand what's happening if they call in and you aren't available to help; and
- If someone else has to take over the issue, for whatever reason, then they're not starting from the beginning thanks to a history of what has already been done in trying to fix the problem.

Tip 5: Make it easier for your service desk agents to work

Knowledge management, if implemented effectively, can reduce call fix times, reduce incidents and empower the service desk. By capturing and sharing knowledge over time and organising it by support level tier (first line, second line, and so on), service desk agents can be provided with a helpful source of knowledge that can make their job easier.

Tip 6: Check your customer's previously logged incidents

Taking a moment to quickly review a customer's previously logged tickets can save a lot of time and also prevent the same questions from being asked or the same solutions from being tried, again (and again).

For recurring issues, problem management can be initiated to establish a root cause, and actions devised to prevent them from happening again.

Tip 7: Take advantage of remote support capabilities

Technological advances mean that remote support can promptly address issues by ensuring the investigation and fix, or the installation of new software, are done there and then.

Exploit remote support technologies as much as possible, in conjunction with live chat if available. It's more cost-effective than desk-side support, and also delivers a better customer experience as it lets IT support personnel handle multiple customers and issues concurrently.

Tip 8: Escalate if needed

Asking for help or escalating issues in a timely fashion ensures that the issue gets the level of seniority needed to resolve it appropriately. ITIL states that the goal of incident management is to fix faults as quickly as possible, with as little adverse impact as possible.[4]

Tip 9: Take ownership

Remember, whatever happens, no matter how long the incident is open for, or which support team it lands with, the service desk will always retain ownership of the incident because it is the point of contact between the customer and the rest of IT.

Honesty, transparency and accountability are three of the most important traits for service desk agents, and demonstrating these to the customer shows that the service desk is doing everything in its power to resolve the issue or to deliver the request.

Career path and certifications

After a couple of years, the daily routine of a service desk agent can feel mundane and demotivating, especially if the environment is not dynamic. Career progression is always the first and foremost thought in the mind of anyone with a reasonable sense of ambition.

An example of such a progression would be from service desk agent to service desk supervisor or manager. From here on and after obtaining relevant intermediate level certifications, individuals can also move into more specialised roles such as incident manager, problem

---

[4] For more information about incident management, see *www.itgovernance.co.uk/blog/the-ultimate-guide-to-itil-incident-management*.

manager, change manager, etc. eventually reaching up to the level of a service delivery manager and beyond. For those with fire in their belly, the sky is the limit for progress.

Some of the mainstream ITSM job roles can be seen on the AXELOS® website.[5]

Certifications for individuals

As far as a service desk agent is concerned, and I have recommended this to my own teams, a change of department or even organisation once every 2–3 years is a good idea to help progress their careers. Gaining certifications along the way will help fast-track this.

To begin with, the ITIL Foundation certification is a must for those employed in an organisation that has embraced the ITIL framework or is in the process of doing so.[6]

Another service management approach that helps service providers create a flexible operating model to deliver desired services and business outcome is VeriSM™.[7] In the VeriSM™ approach, governance is central to every activity, whilst maintaining a strong focus on value, outcomes and the organisational goals. Service management principles are then defined for areas including

---

[5] *www.axelos.com/certifications/career-paths/itsm-careers-path.*

[6] *www.axelos.com/certifications/itil-certifications/itil-foundation.*

[7] *https://verism.global/.*

security, risk, quality and use of assets, and then communicated to all of the staff who are involved with the development and operation of products and services. This approach offers various certification options to individuals.[8]

With advancement in their careers, service desk supervisors or managers may also choose to pursue advanced level certifications in ITIL or other frameworks used within their respective organisations.[9]

CompTIA A+ provides a path for the more technically inclined, covering a range of support skills including operating systems, hardware and networking troubleshooting, and security, among others.[10]

That being said, there are also soft skills that individuals could look to learn and apply in their daily work, such as *critical thinking* and *emotional intelligence*. There are many affordable options online to acquire these skills, such as Udemy, Coursera, edx to name a few.[11]

Certification for the service desk unit

While individual certifications help improve the overall efficiency of the service desk agent, there are certifications

---

[8] *www.exin.com/verism/professionals/*.

[9] *www.axelos.com/certifications/itil-certifications*.

[10] *www.comptia.org/certifications/a*.

[11] For more information, see: *www.udemy.com/*, *www.coursera.org/*, *www.edx.org/*.

available that will take the service desk to the next level and add value to the organisation as a whole.

SDI's Service Desk Certification is the only industry standard-based accreditation programme designed specifically to certify service desk quality.[12] This provides a set of clear and measurable benchmarks for IT service operations.

ISO/IEC 20000 is the international ITSM standard that enables IT departments to ensure that their ITSM processes are aligned to international best practices.[13] It also helps organisations benchmark how they deliver managed services, measure service levels and assess their performance.

Common terms explained

More often than not, while implementing best practices it also helps to have a basic understanding of the most common terms associated with everyday operations. As far as a service desk is concerned, below are a few examples of such terms and their definitions.

Alert:

An alert is the notification of an unexpected change in the state of a configuration item or service within the IT environment against defined thresholds and controls

---

[12] *www.servicedeskinstitute.com/service-desk-benchmarking/service-desk-certification/*.

[13] *www.itgovernance.co.uk/iso20000*.

representing 'normal operations'. An alert will lead to the creation of an incident.

Case:

A case is the incident or request record created within the ITSM tool. The case is the mechanism for documenting the symptoms, classification and prioritisation of each incident and recording actions taken through to resolution.

Event:

An event is an unexpected change in the state of a configuration item or service within the IT environment. An event can, but might not always, lead to the creation of an incident.

Incident:

An incident is defined as an unplanned interruption to an IT service or a reduction in the quality of an IT service. Failure of a configuration item that has not yet impacted service should also be considered an incident.

Known error:

A known error is the record of a fault in a configuration item or service, which has been diagnosed through problem management and RCA. Typically, a known error record will provide a temporary workaround for recurring incidents until a permanent fix has been implemented.

Major incident:

A major incident is an incident that is usually categorised as priority 1 or priority 2, in accordance with the incident prioritisation matrix defined within the incident management process.

Problem:

A problem is the underlying cause of one or more incidents.

Solution:

Solutions are records of repeatable steps to resolve recurring incidents, incidents of a similar nature within the IT environment or answers to common questions received by the service desk. Typically, a solution will not be associated to a problem; however, the use of solutions supports the identification or problems through proactive analysis.

Workaround:

A set of immediate steps provided to the service desk, which offers an alternative method of achieving the desired action/state or recovery of service. Workarounds should not involve complex re-engineering of business process and should be deemed acceptable to the customer.

Critical system:

A system defined as critical to the functioning of the organisation, within the service catalogue.

Non-critical system:

Any provision of IT to the business by the internal IT service that is not considered critical to the functioning of the organisation. Such systems may be defined within the service catalogue.

Root cause analysis – overview

RCA is the process of identifying the cause of a problem, which, when solutions are acted upon to remove, change or control the causes, ensure the problem does not recur.

Cause is a combination of actions and conditions that, when they exist at a relative point in time, result in an effect. Each cause is itself an effect of a further combination of actions and conditions. The objective of an RCA is to map through levels of cause and effect until all possible causes are exhausted or a set of causes are identified that can be removed or controlled to prevent the problem from recurring.

The various steps involved in RCA are:

- **Problem definition – a problem can be defined by identifying:**
  - o Primary effect (what happened);
  - o Business impact; and
  - o Known causes.
- **Analysis** – The analysis stage identifies cause-and-effect relationships. Every effect must be preceded by at least one action and one condition, both regarded as causes. The combination of the action(s) and conditions(s) at a common point of space and time

results in the effect. The actions and conditions should be documented as causes of the primary effect.

Each cause is then considered an effect with a preceding set of causes (actions and conditions). The relationship of these preceding causes is examined and documented.

This process is continued until the cause and effect relationships are fully exhausted and a controllable set of causes is identified. The resulting mapping of all the cause and effect relationships in the analysis stage creates a logical tree for the problem.

- **Solutions** – The purpose of this stage is to develop a sequence of remedial activities to isolate the root cause and prevent a recurrence of the problem.

  Each cause identified within the root cause needs to be rated in terms of impact to the problem and probability of recurrence in order to assist in prioritisation of any subsequent solutions.

  Each remedial activity (action taken) can be classified into the categories outlined in Table 8 to assist in delegation of ownership.

Table 8: Categories of Ownership Delegation

Category	Description
Process	A weakness, failure or unexpected result in the execution of procedures used.
People	Gaps in skills and knowledge within teams and individuals responsible.
Application	Unexpected or non-compliant functioning of business IT applications.
Infrastructure	Unexpected or non-compliant functioning of IT infrastructure or platforms.
Supplier	Actions that can only be addressed through support of a third-party vendor.

Root cause analysis methods

There are different approaches that can be taken to conduct RCA sessions, some of which are described below.

Causal relationship mapping

Causal relationship mapping works on the assumption that every cause has at least one corresponding action and one corresponding condition.

The process asks the question 'caused by?' for each action and condition, treating each as an effect of the earlier cause. Causes are evidenced where possible. This is performed until all causes are exhausted or a controllable cause is identified.

Challenges

The method requires strong facilitation to break down barriers in expertise and ownership. All stakeholders need to feel involved in order to achieve the full perspective of the problem and reach an agreed view. The method can be time-consuming as it often raises questions that need further research before the next causal relationship can be identified.

Ishikawa (fishbone) diagrams

This method originates from manufacturing and involves brainstorming possible causes and assigning them to defined categories, which helps to identify variation between possible causes.

When the brainstorming is concluded, participants vote on the most likely causes, and solutions are determined to prevent these 'root causes'.

Fishbone diagrams can be useful for complex problems. They encourage creative thinking and can lead to an exhaustive list of possible conditions that contribute to the root cause. This method has proven effective in industries and scenarios where the expected result is predictable and there is normally little variance in the underlying process and system behaviour.

Challenges

Fishbone diagrams help identify possible causes of the problem, but not the causal relationships between these causes. While the method encourages thinking, it risks a high degree of subjective analysis (based on little evidence).

Pareto analysis

The Pareto principle presumes that 80% of problems are caused by 20% of causes.[14] Pareto analysis applies a statistical approach to RCA. It uses a database of problems to identify the common causal factors and characteristics within the business that are related to the problems.

Pareto analysis is effective when there is a large sample set of data relating to the problem or a group of problems. It helps determine where problem solving should start from. Pareto analysis is typically used to refine the scope of a problem before the root cause is analysed using other tools and methods.

Challenges

The accuracy of Pareto analysis is dependent on the size and quality of the data set. The process focuses on common trends without examining causal relationships or key patterns outside of the data, which can lead to too many conditions or the wrong condition being addressed.

---

[14] *www.forbes.com/sites/kevinkruse/2016/03/07/80-20-rule/#4f70f983814b*.

5 Whys

5 Whys is a simple technique performed by asking why a cause occurred, five times, to arrive at a single controllable cause.[15]

It is effective when used on minor problems that require little more than discussion of the event.

Challenges

5 Whys identifies causal relationships only in a linear manner. This could lead to preconceived opinions being inaccurately 'proven' to be the root cause and may only identify a single action or condition of the root cause.

---

[15] www.revolutionlearning.co.uk/5-whys-problem-solving-technique/.

CHAPTER 10: CONCLUSION

Finally, we have reached the end of this book. As mentioned at the beginning, its sole purpose is to ease the implementation of a fully functional service desk complete with efficient and trained agents and the necessary processes, procedures and related documentation. As with all such endeavors, how much of it to absorb and adapt is left to the discretion of the readers as this usually varies from organisation to organisation and individuals that form part of service desks.

Overall, I hope I have been able to do justice to the purpose stated above. I look forward to comments and reviews on how effective this book has been in bringing about a structure in service desk operations within your organisation. Perhaps, there might even be a need for a sequel.

All the same, I hope you have enjoyed the ride!

FURTHER READING

IT Governance Publishing (ITGP) is the world's leading publisher for governance and compliance. Our industry-leading pocket guides, books, training resources and toolkits are written by real-world practitioners and thought leaders. They are used globally by audiences of all levels, from students to C-suite executives.

Our high-quality publications cover all IT governance, risk and compliance frameworks and are available in a range of formats. This ensures our customers can access the information they need in the way they need it.

Our other publications about service desk management include:

- *The Universal Service Desk (USD) – Implementing, controlling and improving service delivery* by Brian Johnson and Léon-Paul de Rouw, *www.itgovernancepublishing.co.uk/product/the-universal-service-desk-usd*
- *ITIL® Foundation Essentials ITIL 4 Edition – The ultimate revision guide, second edition* by Claire Agutter, *www.itgovernancepublishing.co.uk/product/itil-foundation-essentials-itil-4-edition-the-ultimate-revision-guide-second-edition*
- *ITIL® 4 Essentials – Your essential guide for the ITIL 4 Foundation exam and beyond, second edition* by Claire Agutter, *www.itgovernancepublishing.co.uk/product/itil-4-*

*essentials-your-essential-guide-for-the-itil-4-
foundation-exam-and-beyond-second-edition*

For more information on ITGP and branded publishing services, and to view our full list of publications, visit www.itgovernancepublishing.co.uk.

To receive regular updates from ITGP, including information on new publications in your area(s) of interest, sign up for our newsletter at *www.itgovernancepublishing.co.uk/topic/newsletter*.

Branded publishing

Through our branded publishing service, you can customise ITGP publications with your company's branding.

Find out more at

www.itgovernancepublishing.co.uk/topic/branded-publishing-services.

Related services

ITGP is part of GRC International Group, which offers a comprehensive range of complementary products and services to help organisations meet their objectives.

For a full range of resources on ITIL visit *www.itgovernance.co.uk/shop/category/itil*.

Training services

The IT Governance training programme is built on our extensive practical experience designing and implementing management systems based on ISO standards, best practice and regulations.

Our courses help attendees develop practical skills and comply with contractual and regulatory requirements. They also support career development via recognised qualifications.

Learn more about our training courses and view the full course catalogue at *www.itgovernance.co.uk/training*.

Professional services and consultancy

We are a leading global consultancy of IT governance, risk management and compliance solutions. We advise businesses around the world on their most critical issues and present cost-saving and risk-reducing solutions based on international best practice and frameworks.

We offer a wide range of delivery methods to suit all budgets, timescales and preferred project approaches.

Find out how our consultancy services can help your organisation at *www.itgovernance.co.uk/consulting*.

Industry news

Want to stay up to date with the latest developments and resources in the IT governance and compliance market? Subscribe to our Weekly Round-up newsletter and we will send you mobile-friendly emails with fresh news and features about your preferred areas of interest, as well as unmissable offers and free resources to help you successfully start your projects. *www.itgovernance.co.uk/weekly-round-up*.

EU for product safety is Stephen Evans, The Mill Enterprise Hub, Stagreenan, Drogheda, Co. Louth, A92 CD3D, Ireland. (servicecentre@itgovernance.eu)

www.ingramcontent.com/pod-product-compliance
Lightning Source LLC
Chambersburg PA
CBHW070841070326
40690CB00009B/1641